The Catholic BIBLE

for Children

Ignatius

MAGNIFICAT.

THE AUTHORS

Karine-Marie Amiot, the mother of a family and the author of many children's books, writes regularly for the children's press.

François Carmagnac, a priest passionate about the Bible, enjoys reading and telling Bible stories. He is in charge of pastoral services for the young, for high-school students, and for the eighteen-to-thirty age group of his diocese.

Christophe Raimbault, a graduate of the French Biblical and Archeological School of Jerusalem, is a parish priest and youth pastor. He is a commentator of the Bible, heads his diocesan house of vocations, and is a teaching assistant at the Catholic Institute of Paris, France.

Translated by Janet Chevrier.

ILLUSTRATIONS
Andrée Bienfait

Nihil obstat: Rev. Msgr. Michael F. Hull
Imprimatur: ✠ Most Reverend Dennis J. Sullivan
             Vicar General of New York
             June 6, 2011

To the parents:

"Let the children come to me . . ."

Open, taste, see: that is what a true Bible for children invites us to do.

While written for the young, the brief, clear texts in *The Catholic Bible for Children* have lost nothing of the savor and richness of Scripture. They are accompanied, moreover, by vivid illustrations, rich in color and detail, that bring them to life.

Read this Bible to your children, or let them read it to you; let the youngest ones narrate the pictures to you. Together, let yourselves be carried along by the spirit and the liveliness of these stories.

Through these events and heroes, some well-known, some less familiar, share the extraordinary adventure of this small group of people who walked with God, became his friends, and made a covenant with him.

Rediscover Jesus with your children; let them come listen to him. Jesus loved to speak to children. His words were meant for them, too.

His were words that tell of love, that speak of joy—words of the past, of the present, and of the future, words that help us to know God and to live together in happiness.

The authors

CONTENTS

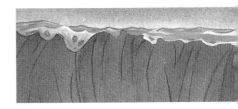

CHAPTER 4

WHEN GOD SPOKE TO HIS PEOPLE

CHAPTER 5

WHEN GOD SENT HIS SON, JESUS

CHAPTER 9
WHEN JESUS GAVE HIS LIFE FOR US

CHAPTER 10
WHEN THE SPIRIT OF GOD SENDS A MISSION

Chapter 1

When God Created Heaven and Earth

The Creation of the World

Genesis 1:1—2:4

God decided to create the world. He said,
"Let there be light!" And there was light!
He called the light "day" and the darkness "night".
It was the first day.

"God said, 'Let there be light!'" (Genesis 1:3)

God separated the sky from the land and the sea. He covered the land with plants and flowers and fruit trees. He created the sun and the stars and placed them in the sky to shine over the earth. He filled the world with living creatures: the birds of the air, the fish of the seas, and all the animals of the land.

"And there was evening and there was morning." (Genesis 1:19)

God did not overlook the wild beasts or the desert animals or even the bugs in the fields! From the ant to the elephant, God created every kind of living creature. Finally, God decided to create man. "Your name is Adam", he said. "I give this wonderful garden to you. Farm the soil, and take care of the earth I have created." Adam ruled over all the animals.

But God did not want Adam to be alone. So he created woman. Adam named her Eve. Their life in this wonderful garden was to be full of delights. It would make them happy to show God all the joy in their hearts.

On the seventh day, God was pleased with his work, and he rested.

Adam and Eve

Genesis 2:4—3:24

Adam and Eve had everything they needed to be happy forever. God said to them, "Eat all that you like, except the fruit of the tree of the knowledge of good and evil. If you eat that, you will die."

One day, under the tree of the knowledge of good and evil, Eve met a sly and cunning snake. He tempted her.

"Taste this delicious fruit! You will not die. You will become like God." Eve gave in to temptation and ate the forbidden fruit. She gave some to her husband, and he ate it also.

Adam and Eve were afraid God would be angry. They knew they had just disobeyed him very badly. So when they heard God's footsteps coming toward them, they hid. "What have you done?" God asked. And he made Adam and Eve leave the beautiful garden.

Cain and Abel

Genesis 4:1–16

Adam and Eve had two children: Cain and Abel. Cain tilled the soil. Abel was a shepherd. When the brothers brought gifts to God, Cain gave some of his grain, while Abel gave the best of his flock. God saw that Abel gave the better gift and was more pleased with him than with Cain. And Cain was jealous of Abel. One day, in a fit of anger, Cain attacked Abel and killed him.

God asked Cain, "Where is your brother?" Cain lied, "I do not know." But God said to him, "I know you killed your brother. This is a grave sin! You must leave my presence." Cain was very afraid. But even though he had to wander the earth, God promised to protect him.

"Where is Abel your brother?... What have you done?" (Genesis 4:9–10)

Noah's Ark

Genesis 6:5—9:17

The wickedness of men spread everywhere over the earth. "Enough!" said God. He went to see Noah, the only good man, and told him, "Build a huge boat. I am going to cover the earth with water to drown all of this wickedness."

So Noah built an ark out of wood. Then, as God had told him to do, Noah entered the ark with his whole family, and he brought on board two of every kind of living creature of the land and the sky. Then God closed the door of the ark.

The rain began to fall. It was a flood!

"Come into the ark." (Genesis 6:18)

The rain continued to fall for a long, long time! Water covered the whole earth right up to the mountaintops, and the ark floated.

After forty days, when the rain stopped, Noah sent a dove off into the sky. It soon returned with an olive branch in its beak. "Hurray, there must be dry land!"

"I set my bow in the cloud, and it shall be a sign of the covenant between me and the earth." (Genesis 9:13)

The animals leaped out of the ark. The children ran in the fresh green grass. The earth smelled good. It was fit for life again. The sun shone, and a rainbow stretched like a bridge between heaven and earth. It was a sign:

"God promised me there would never again be such a flood. Now we can live in peace", said Noah.

The Tower of Babel

Genesis 11:1–9

Noah's children had many children, and their children's children had many, many more! They all talked together and decided to build a huge tower right up to the sky. They took themselves for heroes or even gods! Nothing seemed impossible to them!

God decided to put a stop to this. He said,
"Let each of them speak a different language!"
From that moment on, they could no longer understand
each other. They gave up building the tower and
scattered to the four corners of the earth. The building
they abandoned is called the tower of Babel.

Abraham and Isaac

Genesis 12:1–5; 15:3–7; 18:1–15; 21:1–7

Abraham was a friend of God. One day,
God called to him, "Leave your country, and go to
the land that I will show you." Abraham took his wife,
Sarah, and his whole family and walked a very long time.
One evening, he at last pitched his tent under some oak trees:
"Look, Sarah, this land is for us and for our children."
But Sarah was sad because she was old and had no children.

It was noon. Abraham saw three travelers in the distance. "Sarah! Quick, bake some bread! We have visitors!" The three travelers rested under an oak tree. "In one year", one of them said, "you will have a baby." Sarah laughed, "That's impossible, we're too old!" "Nothing is impossible for God", answered the traveler.

"Your descendants will be as numerous as the stars." (see Genesis 15:5)

God kept his promise. Sarah was expecting a baby!
Abraham was wild with joy! Soon, the baby
was born—he smiled and was full of life. "Little boy,
your name is Isaac, which means 'God smiles'."
Isaac grew up and became a man. He had two sons:
Jacob and Esau.

Joseph and His Brothers

Genesis 37:12–28

Then Jacob in turn grew up. He had twelve sons! He loved one of the younger sons, Joseph, more than the others and made him a special coat.

"He's our father's favorite", his older brothers grumbled to each other.

Joseph's brothers never stopped making fun of him and playing nasty tricks on him.

One day, they were so jealous they threw him to the bottom of a well. But when a caravan of Egyptian traders came by, they thought, "Let's pull Joseph out of the well and sell him to the traders! . . . And good riddance!"

Jacob was in despair: he thought Joseph was dead.
But God watched over him. Joseph became
the friend of Pharaoh, the king of Egypt.

When a great famine came upon the land,
Joseph took charge of distributing food.
When his brothers came to Egypt to buy food,
he recognized them in the crowd. He forgave them
for everything, and Joseph's brothers moved to Egypt
with their wives, their children, and all their servants.
This big family became the Hebrew people.

Chapter 2

When God
Set His People Free

Moses
Saved from the Water

Exodus 1:1—2:10

Pharaoh was worried: "There are too many of these
Hebrews living in our country! One day, they could make
war on us…We must force them to work for us
without pay!" Even as slaves the Hebrews grew in number,
so Pharaoh ordered that their newborn sons be killed.
What a terrible panic! Egyptian soldiers broke into
all the houses and carried off the babies!

"I have seen the affliction of my people who are in Egypt." (Exodus 3:7)

To save her infant son, one Hebrew mother
hid her baby in a basket and placed it on the river.
A princess was bathing there with her servants.
Suddenly, she saw the basket floating on the water!
"Oh, a tiny little baby! I'll take care of you.
I will call you Moses, because that means
'saved from the water'."

Moses and Pharaoh

Exodus 2:11–15; 3; 7:14—11:10

Moses grew up. He knew how miserable his people were in Egypt. One day, he saw a soldier beating a Hebrew. In a fit of rage, Moses killed the soldier. The next day, the whole town had heard about it.

Moses was betrayed! Fearing Pharaoh's anger, he ran far away into the desert, where he became a shepherd. In the mountains, he once saw a fire in the middle of a bush, but the bush itself did not burn up. Moses went to look at it.

A voice said, "I am the God of Abraham, Isaac, and Jacob. I have seen how my people are mistreated. Go to Egypt, rescue them, and lead them to the beautiful land that I will give you. I will help you, Moses, and I will always be with you."

Moses went to see Pharaoh and begged, "Let my people go!" Pharaoh refused. He just laughed at him. Moses insisted, but Pharaoh was hardhearted and would not give in.

When God saw Pharaoh's stubbornness, he sent ten plagues on Egypt: frogs, flies, locusts, disease . . .

Pharaoh would not give in until his own son died in the final plague, which passed over the homes of the Hebrews. Awaiting their freedom, the Hebrews shared a hurried meal of roasted lamb and unleavened bread.
At last Pharaoh allowed the Hebrews to leave. Quickly they loaded their baggage onto carts.
God had kept his promise!

"It is the LORD's Passover."
(Exodus 12:11)

The Crossing of the Red Sea

Exodus 12:1–11; 13:17–22; 14:5—15:21

In the night, the huge caravan of Hebrews set off on their departure from Egypt. Moses led the way. He did not know what was going to happen, but he trusted in God. Their journey was to last a very long time. It is called the "exodus".

"Watch out! Look behind us! Pharaoh has changed his mind! The Egyptian soldiers are coming after us…!"

With all their children and their baggage, the Hebrews could not go any faster! They trembled with fear. In front of them was the sea; behind them, the Egyptians. They were trapped!

Moses called out to God for help.
Then he advanced toward the sea and
raised his walking stick before the waters…
and the sea split in two!

A great passage opened up before him…
And the long caravan of Hebrews crossed the sea on dry land.

The Egyptians had almost caught up with them when, suddenly, the sea closed and crashed over them. The Egyptians were swallowed up under the waves along with their chariots and all their horses. On the other shore, the Hebrews were safe. They sang of the wonders of God. They celebrated and danced to the sound of their tambourines.

"Thus the LORD saved Israel that day."
(Exodus 14:30)

The March through the Desert

Exodus 15:22—17:7

The people marched through the desert. It was hot! Everyone was hungry and thirsty. They accused Moses of leading them to their death. Moses called on God for help. "Do not be afraid; I am with you always", God answered him. Every morning, God sent them a strange kind of bread called "manna". Moses struck a rock with his walking stick, and water gushed out. The people ate and drank.

Quails fell from the sky. "These little birds are for you. Eat them!" said God.

The people had everything they needed to eat and drink, but the caravan moved on more and more slowly. The people were tired. They grew weary of not knowing where they were going and of eating the same food every day.

Some people went on complaining. They accused Moses, "It's all because of you that we left Egypt. We trusted you, but we should never have listened! Life is too hard here!" From morning to evening, the people brought Moses their problems and disputes. Moses needed wisdom. So he went off to the mountain to pray to God.

"Why do you put the LORD to the test?"
(Exodus 17:2)

The Ten Commandments

Exodus 19–20; Deuteronomy 5

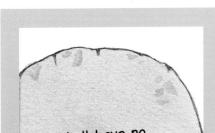

You shall have no other gods besides me.

You shall not make for yourself a graven image ... or bow down to them.

You shall not take the name of the LORD your God in vain.

Remember the Sabbath day, to keep it holy.

Honor your father and your mother.

Right at the top of Mount Sinai, Moses saw white smoke and heard the voice of God reassuring him, "Do not be afraid, Moses, I am still here. Continue to lead my people. Go back to them. Tell them to have faith."

"It is I who brought you out of Egypt. I am with you forever."

Then God said to Moses, "Tell my people: If you obey my voice and keep my commandments, you will be my own special people. You will be a holy nation."

And God gave Moses his commandments, written on stone tablets, which taught the people to love God and their neighbor.

"The Ten Commandments"
(Exodus 20:1–17)

You shall not kill.

You shall not commit adultery.*

You shall not steal.

You shall not bear false witness.

You shall not covet* anything that belongs to your neighbor.

* To commit adultery means to be unfaithful to your husband or your wife

* To covet means to want to possess something that does not belong to you

The Golden Calf

Exodus 32; 35:1–3

As he was coming down the mountain, Moses saw the people in the distance: "What have they done? They've made themselves a god they can see and touch. They're dancing like madmen around a calf made of gold!" Moses grew angry and destroyed the golden calf. Then he went back to God to plead for forgiveness for his people.

The people went on walking through the desert every day except for every seventh day; on that day, they would rest. Moses placed the tablets of the law in a large and costly chest: the Ark of the Covenant. As they marched along, men carried it at the head of the caravan. On their days of rest, they placed it in a tent where everyone could go to meet and pray to the Lord.

"Behold. I make a covenant." (Exodus 34:10)

The Promised Land

Joshua 1:1–3; Deuteronomy 34

Their travels were over! The caravan had reached the end
of its journey. After wandering for forty years through
the desert, the Hebrew people had found the Promised Land,
a beautiful and fertile land flowing with milk and honey.

Just before their arrival, the aged Moses died. He had fulfilled his mission. The Hebrew people were happy to enter and settle this new country.

Chapter 3

When God Gave His People the Promised Land

The Trumpets of Jericho

Joshua 6:1–20

The Hebrews had arrived in the country of Canaan, the land God had promised them. But they were not welcomed in the cities! To live there, they would have to do battle. In Jericho, all the people marched around the city walls with loud cries. Those carrying the Ark of the Covenant led the way. Men blew their trumpets with all their might, and at the sound of these horns, the walls came tumbling down. "Jericho is ours!" shouted the people. And they moved into the city.

Samson and Delilah

Judges 16:4–31

The Hebrews were at war against
the Philistines. Samson fought on the side
of his people, the Hebrews.

The secret of his great strength was his
long hair. But he fell in love with an enemy
woman: Delilah. And Delilah was cunning!

One night while Samson was sleeping, she cut his hair to take away his strength. The Philistines took advantage of his weakness and blinded him! But Samson's hair grew again. He prayed to God and regained all his strength. He pulled down the columns of the temple, and the Philistines were crushed under the stones.
Samson was victorious.

"O LORD God, . . . strengthen me." (Judges 16:28)

Samuel

1 Samuel 3

Samuel was the helper of Eli, the old guardian of the temple. One night, Samuel could not get to sleep. Suddenly, he gave a start. A voice was calling him: "Samuel, Samuel!"

So he went to Eli and said, "You called me?"

"Speak, for your servant hears." (1 Samuel 3:10)

"No, it wasn't I. It was surely the Lord speaking to you. Try to sleep, and if he calls you again, answer, 'Here I am.'" Samuel was not at all sleepy anymore. Suddenly, he gave another start. A voice was again calling him: "Samuel, Samuel!" "This time", thought Samuel, "I know it is God who is speaking to me." He jumped right out of bed and answered, "Here I am, Lord!" Samuel grew up, always listening to the word of God.

David and His Brothers

1 Samuel 16:1–13

One day, God sent Samuel to see Jesse: "I have chosen the future king from among his sons." Jesse called seven of his sons and presented them to Samuel one by one. The only one missing was David, the youngest, who was out tending the sheep.

"But David is just the one I want to see!"
Samuel said to Jesse. "Send for him!"

Samuel placed his hand on David's head, saying,
"David, it is you who will be king of Israel."

"The Spirit of the LORD came mightily
upon David from that day forward."
(1 Samuel 16:13)

David and Goliath

1 Samuel 17

The Hebrews and the Philistines were at war again. David heard the voice of Goliath, the Philistine giant, thunder, "Is there no one willing to fight me?"

"Yes, I will!" answered David. "I know I'm only little, but with God's help, I'll be stronger than you!" David was clever: he took along his slingshot and stones, with which he had protected his sheep against lions and bears. Goliath came toward him with his great sword. David prayed to God. He took his slingshot and hurled a stone at the giant's forehead. Goliath fell dead to the ground. "By the grace of God, I have won!" shouted David.

David and the Ark of the Covenant

2 Samuel 5:6–12

David grew up and was a good king to all his people. He made his home in the most beautiful city in his country, perched right on top of a hill. The city of King David is called Jerusalem, which means "the city of peace".

David had the Ark of the Covenant brought up to Jerusalem. He made merry and danced before the Ark: "Now God inhabits my city. Yes, God is truly present in Jerusalem!"

David and Bathsheba

2 Samuel 11–1

David fell in love with a beautiful young woman named Bathsheba. But Bathsheba was already married to Uriah, which made David so jealous! One evening, he decided to get rid of Uriah! "Let's have him sent to war", he ordered, "and place him in the front line of the battle. I want him killed so that Bathsheba can be mine."

Uriah obeyed King David's orders. He went off to war and was killed in combat. David was glad: "Now Bathsheba will be my wife!" But God sent him a messenger, Nathan: "David, your sin is very evil!" David was ashamed. He shut himself in his room and refused to see anyone. David was truly sorry for what he had done. He begged God's forgiveness, and God forgave David. He gave him and Bathsheba a son, whom they named Solomon.

David and Solomon

Psalms

David and his son Solomon prayed to God. Before the Ark of the Covenant, Solomon listened to his father teach him about the love and the wisdom of God. Together they sang psalms. These are beautiful prayers, like poems, to tell God everything deep in the heart of man: "I thank you", "Forgive me", "I beg you", "I am afraid", "Help me", "I praise you", "I love you."

The Building of the Jerusalem Temple

1 Kings 6; 2 Samuel 7

Solomon became king in his turn. He wanted to build a house for God in Jerusalem. He had a huge temple constructed and the Ark of the Covenant placed in the center. The people came often to the Temple to meet God, because that was where God lived.

"O LORD,
our Lord,
how majestic
is your name
in all the earth!"

"You whose glory
above the heavens
is chanted
by the mouth of
babies and infants."
(Psalm 8)

The Judgment
of Solomon

1 Kings 3:16–28

One day, two women came to see Solomon.
They were fighting over a baby, each claiming:
"He's mine!" "No, you're a liar! He's mine!"

Solomon considered their case like a wise and just king and put them to a test. "I see no other solution: divide the baby in two!" One of the women agreed. The other refused, crying, "No! You can give her the baby! But do not kill him!" That was how Solomon knew she was the baby's real mother. He gave the child to her, saying, "Take good care of him. I know now how much you love him."

The Queen of Sheba

1 Kings 10; 2 Chronicles 9

Like his father, David, Solomon was a very good king. Fame of his great wisdom spread well beyond his country. Kings and princes came from far and wide to meet him. One day, Solomon received a visit from the queen of Sheba. She made a very long journey with all of her servants to seek his counsel and advice, so great was his renown. She brought him jewels and spices and questioned him about many matters. "Never before", she said, "have I seen such a wise and just king. Blessed are your people!"

"Happy are [those] who ... hear your wisdom."
(1 Kings 10:8)

Chapter 4

When God Spoke
to His People

The Prophets

The people of the kingdom of Israel were constantly at war with each other and fighting with their neighbors. God sent messengers, the prophets, to denounce all this evil and to reassure the people. They all carried the same message, "Stop your wicked ways, and listen to your God." God chose several prophets: Elijah, Elisha, Jeremiah, Hosea, Amos, Daniel, Jonah, Isaiah . . .

"I have been most zealous for the Lord."
(see 1 Kings 19:10)

Elijah and the Tiny Whisper

1 Kings 19

The prophet Elijah worked many wonders in the service of God. One day, some people who did not like what he had done threatened to kill him. Elijah became afraid and fled to the mountains. Suddenly a great storm began to blow... but God was not in the wind. There was a terrible earthquake and a fire ... but God was not in them. Then, there was silence, and Elijah heard God's voice in a tiny whisper: "What are you doing here, Elijah?" Elijah told him of his fears, and God promised to help him.

Elijah and Elisha

2 Kings 2; 5:1–14

Elijah was walking with Elisha on the banks of the Jordan River. Elijah was old. He had done everything that God had asked him to do. Without even time to say farewell to his friend, he was suddenly taken up to heaven in a chariot of fire.

As he was going, Elijah let
his prophet's mantle slip to the
ground, as if to say to Elisha,
"Now, this mantle is yours.
It's your turn to continue God's mission."

One day, Naaman, the general of a foreign
army, went to see the prophet Elisha: "I have
leprosy. Only you can heal me." "Wash seven
times in the Jordan", Elisha told him. At first,
Naaman was very disappointed: he had at least
expected the prophet to say some magic words!
How was this to heal him? But his servant
persuaded Naaman to trust Elisha. So he bathed
seven times in the Jordan, and, when he came out,
he was healed!

Jeremiah, Hosea, and Amos

**Jeremiah 18; Hosea 11:1–7;
Amos 2:6–16; 8:4–8**

One day, God asked the prophet
Jeremiah to go visit a potter. As Jeremiah
watched the potter modeling the clay,
he understood that God behaves toward
his people like this potter. He does his
best to make his creation strong and fine.
He takes care of the work of his hands.

Through the prophet Hosea, God told
his people that, no matter how much
they disobeyed him, he loved them as his
children. He told them it was he who had
taught them to walk, carried them in
his arms, and led them with love. It was
he who had fed them and comforted
them with warm and tender compassion.

Through the prophet Amos, God told his people that he had seen merchants cheating customers to make more money. He had seen them lying and disobeying the law. No one paid any attention to the poor and the needy. God gave the people a stern warning: "If you are unjust and selfish, if you don't think of others, you will be punished!"

The Destruction of Jerusalem

2 Kings 24:10–27; 25:1–21

There was discord everywhere. The people of Israel were fighting between themselves and against other countries as well. Soldiers from Babylon captured the king of Judah, the king of the Israelites, and carried off all the treasures of the house of the Lord. They took all the people by force to Babylon. Then they destroyed the city of Jerusalem.

But God did not abandon his people.

Daniel in the Lions' Den

Daniel 6

Daniel, a young man from Israel, was living in Babylon. He often visited King Darius, who greatly admired his intelligence. When the king asked him, Daniel would interpret his dreams for him. Some of the royal ministers at the palace became jealous of Daniel and tried to find a way to kill him.

One day, the king's ministers surprised Daniel praying in his room. They reported him to the king: "We saw Daniel! He was praying to the God of his country. That's against the law! He must be punished and thrown into the lions' den."

Darius was deeply saddened: "I am going to lose my friend! But rules are rules … and even the king must respect the law." That evening, just before Daniel was to be thrown into the lions' den, Darius went to see his friend. He begged him,

"Pray to your God to save you."

"May your God … deliver you." (Daniel 6:16)

The next morning, Darius ran to the lions'
den. It was incredible: Daniel was alive!
God had protected him from the wild beasts.
Full of joy, Darius let Daniel out of the den
and, in his place, threw in all of his jealous
ministers. That day, Darius decided to make
a new law: "From now on, throughout all
my kingdom, people shall know that the God
of Daniel is the living God, who rescues
and works wonders."

Jonah in the Belly of the Whale

Jonah

God ordered the prophet Jonah to go to Nineveh.
But Jonah was afraid to go to that great city.
It was said that the people of Nineveh were thieves
and bandits!

Instead of leaving for Nineveh, Jonah disobeyed God and jumped onto a ship to flee in the opposite direction.

Suddenly, the wind rose at sea. There was a howling storm! The waves crashed over the boat. The sailors trembled with fear. "It's my fault", shouted Jonah. "God is angry with me. He has sent this great tempest because I disobeyed him! Throw me into the sea!"

The sailors threw Jonah overboard. He sank deeper and deeper under the swirling waves, when all at once … a huge fish swallowed him up! And right away, the storm calmed.

Jonah was trapped in the belly of the fish. For three days and three nights, he prayed and asked God's forgiveness. At last, the fish spat Jonah back out on the shore. He left immediately for Nineveh. He walked for three days through the city proclaiming: "In forty days, Nineveh will be destroyed!" The people of Nineveh believed God and repented. They decided to stop their evil ways, and God forgave them. Jonah was astounded. But God told him: "Should I not pity Nineveh, when there are so many people there?"

"You are a gracious God and merciful." (Jonah 4:2)

The Sufferings of Job

Job

Job was a good and righteous man.
One day, for no reason, he lost everything.
His children died. He fell ill. Even his friends
snubbed him. They whispered behind his
back: "He surely must have done something
very bad to suffer so many tragedies all
at once!" Job wept and was angry. "God!"
he cried, "Come to my aid! Help me!"

Job was sure God heard him: "I have faith that everything will soon get better!" His friends thought he was mad. They said to each other, "There's no doubt about it: God has abandoned him!" But Job did not listen to them. He went on praying and never stopped crying out to God.

At last, God answered him. Job soon regained his health. He had more children and was blessed with much great fortune. He had a new life!

Isaiah and the Promised Savior

Isaiah 9:1–6

The prophet Isaiah brought great hope to the people: "One day, the Savior will come. A child will be born who will become a king forever. He will bring justice, peace, and joy to everyone. He will light up the whole world with his love." The people waited for this child God had promised them.
He would be the Messiah.

Other texts in the Bible, and especially some psalms (see page 68), also promise the coming Messiah:

"Your divine throne endures
for ever and ever.
Your royal scepter is a scepter
of equity; you love righteousness
and hate wickedness.
Therefore God, your God,
has anointed you
with the oil of gladness..."
(Psalm 45)

"The people who walked in darkness
have seen a great light."
(Isaiah 9:2)

Chapter 5

When God
Sent His Son, Jesus

The Annunciation to Mary

Luke 1:26–38; Matthew 1:18–25

Mary grew up in Nazareth. Everyone admired her. She had just become engaged to Joseph, the carpenter. He was of the family of King David. One day, the angel Gabriel was sent to Mary: "Hail, Mary. God has chosen you to be the mother of the Messiah, the one who is to come into the world to save all mankind." Mary was astonished! She could not understand.

So the angel said to her, "Do not be afraid! You will bear a child by the power of God. You will call him Jesus." And Mary said Yes! Then Joseph had a dream. He heard the voice of an angel saying, "Do not be afraid to take Mary as your wife. She will give birth to the Savior by the power of God. You will name him Jesus." And Joseph did as the angel told him.

"Hail, full of grace, the Lord is with you!"
(Luke 1:28)

The Visit to Elizabeth

Luke 1:39–56

The angel Gabriel had told Mary
that her cousin Elizabeth was expecting
a baby, even though she was too old
to bear a child. "For, you see, nothing
is impossible for God", the angel had said.
Mary went in haste to help Elizabeth.
Her child would be called John.

When Elizabeth heard
Mary's greeting, her baby leaped
in her womb. "How blessed you are,
Mary!" said Elizabeth. "The baby
you are carrying is very special indeed!"
Mary smiled: "Yes, my heart rejoices!
My soul sings the wonders of God
for this child who is to be born."

The Birth of Jesus

Luke 2:1–7

The Roman emperor ordered
a great census to count all
the people on earth. Joseph and Mary
set out for Bethlehem, in the land of
Joseph's family. However, it was almost
time for Mary's baby to be born,
and she was tired out
by the long journey.

In Bethlehem, Joseph knocked on every door, trying to find a room, but there was no place left for them anywhere. So Mary and Joseph took shelter in a stable. That night, the child was born. Mary wrapped him up and laid him in the animals' manger.

The Adoration of the Shepherds

Luke 2:8–16

In the fields nearby, shepherds were watching over their flocks in the night. Suddenly, they saw a great light, and they heard the voice of an angel say, "I bring you news of great joy! An extraordinary baby has just been born. He is the Messiah, the One sent from God. Go to see him. You will find him lying in a manger."

The shepherds found Jesus in the stable.
They fell to their knees in wonder at the sight
of the sleeping child who had come
to save all men.

"Glory to God in the highest,
and on earth peace."
(Luke 2:14)

The Adoration of the Magi

Matthew 2:1–12

Far away from Bethlehem, wise men, called Magi, were watching the sky. "A new star is shining! A king has just been born!" The Magi followed the star.

They crossed the desert and arrived in Jerusalem at the palace of King Herod. They asked him, "Where is the new king?"

This worried Herod greatly: "I am the king! If you find another, let me know! I will go visit him, too."

Guided by the star, the Magi came to Bethlehem and found Jesus. They offered him precious gifts. They were warned in a dream not to return to Herod. So they went back home by another route.

"Opening their treasures, they offered him gifts, gold and frankincense and myrrh." (Matthew 2:11)

The Flight into Egypt

Matthew 2:13–18

Herod was afraid a new king would take his place. So he sent soldiers to Bethlehem to kill all the children two years old or younger. An angel warned Joseph, "Quick! Take the child and his mother and flee to Egypt. Herod is jealous—he wants to kill him." So, in the night, Joseph took Mary and Jesus with him and left for Egypt.

Jesus at Nazareth

Matthew 2:19–21; Luke 2:39–40

After Herod died, Mary, Joseph, and
Jesus returned to the village of Nazareth.
It was there that Jesus grew up.
He learned to read and loved to pray to
God. He often watched Joseph working.
In the summer, he would listen
to the rustle of the wind in the wheat fields
and rest in the shade of the olive trees.
Jesus would run with his friends through
the vineyards and munch sweet fruits
and dates and figs and almonds.
What a beautiful land it was!

"The child grew and became strong,
filled with wisdom." (Luke 2:40)

Jesus in the Temple

Luke 2:41–51

When Jesus was twelve, he went with his parents on pilgrimage. They joined the great crowd marching up to the Temple of Jerusalem.

Along the way, they sang the praises of God.

On the way home, Mary suddenly became worried: "Joseph, where is Jesus? I can't find him anywhere." Mary and Joseph asked everyone, but no one had seen him. Jesus had disappeared! They returned to Jerusalem to search for him.

After three days, Mary and Joseph found Jesus in the Temple, conversing with the great religious scholars. With her eyes full of tears, Mary told him, "You frightened us, Jesus! We have been looking for you everywhere for three days." "Why were you so worried?" Jesus replied. "Didn't you know that I had to be in my Father's house?" But he was obedient and returned with his parents to Nazareth.

"Prepare the way of the Lord." (Matthew 3:3)

The Baptism of Jesus

Matthew 3:1–17; John 1:35–39

Jesus' cousin John grew up, too. He was now living and praying in the desert. He was a great prophet, preparing the people for the Savior: "Repent! Change your hearts! The kingdom of God is very near." Crowds of people came to be baptized by John in the waters of the Jordan River.

One day, Jesus, too, came to see John the Baptist to be baptized in the river. When Jesus rose from the water, the heavens opened and a voice was heard, saying, "This is my beloved Son, with whom I am well pleased."

"He saw the Spirit of God descending like a dove and alighting on him."
(Matthew 3:16)

A little later, Jesus saw some men following him.
He turned and asked them, "What are you seeking?"
"Teacher", they answered, "where are you staying?"
And Jesus said to them, "Come and see."

Chapter 6

When Jesus Visited His People

Jesus in the Synagogue of Nazareth

Luke 4:16–30; Luke 5:1–3

One day in Nazareth, Jesus entered
the synagogue, the Jewish house of prayer.
After reading a passage from the prophet Isaiah,
he said before the whole assembly,
"God promised to send a Savior. Well, today,
God has kept his promise." But they refused
to listen to him: "Isn't that Joseph's son?
He thinks he's the Messiah!"

Another day, by the lake of Gennesaret,*
the crowds thronged to Jesus. Everyone
wanted to hear him and see him.
So Jesus got into a boat and moved a little way
from the shore. Then he spoke to them about God,
who loves all men and wants to be their friend.

*Also known as the Sea of Galilee

The Call of Peter and Andrew

Mark 1:16–20

On the shore, Jesus saw two fishermen, Andrew and Peter, casting their nets. Jesus called them, "Andrew, Peter, leave your nets. Come, follow me!"

"Immediately they left their nets and followed him." (Mark 1:18)

The Call of Matthew

Matthew 9:9

Matthew was a tax collector. Jesus saw him seated at his desk. He said to him, "Matthew, follow me." Matthew stopped his work, got up, and left his business to follow Jesus. And thus Jesus chose twelve friends, his apostles, to help him proclaim the good news of God.

The Rich Man

Mark 10:17–22

A rich man asked Jesus,
"What must I do to gain
eternal life? I already do
everything the law says."
Jesus told him,
"Give all you have to the poor,
and come, follow me."
"Give everything away?
How could I?"
The rich man went away very sad,
for he had many fine possessions.

"Go, sell what you have, and give to the poor, and you will have treasure in heaven." (Mark 10:21)

The Sinful Woman

Luke 7:36–50

An important man named Simon
invited Jesus to supper. Simon was
proud to have Jesus as his guest.
Suddenly, a woman approached
carrying a flask of perfume
in her hands. She fell on her knees
at Jesus' feet and wept, "I've done
something very bad", she seemed
to be saying. "Forgive me."

She bathed his feet with the perfume
and kissed them. Then Jesus said
to her, "I forgive you. Go in peace."
Simon was astonished. So Jesus
explained to him, "You see, Simon,
I have forgiven all her sins because
her heart is full of love."

You Are Peter

Matthew 16:13–20; 10:1–15

Jesus asked his friends, "Who do people say that I am?" Peter answered, "Some think you're John the Baptist. Others say you're a prophet. But I say you are the Son of God." Jesus replied, "Yes, Peter! It is God who has revealed this to you."

Jesus sent his friends
off two by two: "Go out
into the roads. Take nothing
with you: no extra clothes, no sack, no money.
Do not be afraid to enter every house to speak
about God."

The Transfiguration

Matthew 17:1–9

Later, on a mountaintop, Peter, James,
and John saw Jesus become dazzlingly radiant
with the light of God.

"This is my beloved Son: listen to him." (Mark 9:7)

Martha and Mary

Luke 10:38–42

Jesus often went to supper
at Martha and Mary's house.
One evening, Martha was annoyed:
"Mary sits and listens to you for
hours, while I fix dinner all on
my own. Why doesn't she help me?"
But Jesus said to Martha,
"You busy yourself and worry
about many things. Mary chooses
to listen to me. That's what
matters most!"

The Samaritan Woman

John 4:1–15

It was noon, the hottest hour
of the day! The sandy road was hot enough
to burn the feet. Tired out, Jesus
sat down at a well, while his friends
went to the nearest village
to find something to eat. A woman
came to draw water from the well.
Jesus said to her, "I'm thirsty!
Give me a drink…"
And then he offered her a drink as well:
"If you wish, I will give you living water,
and you will never be thirsty again."

"If you knew the gift of God." (John 4:10)

Zaccheus

Luke 19:1–10

Zaccheus collected taxes for the Romans
in Jericho. He was very rich, and people thought
he was dishonest. No one liked him. This day, Jesus
was in Jericho, and a crowd of people rushed to see
him. Zaccheus also wanted to see Jesus, but he was
too short. So he climbed up a tree to get a better view.
Jesus raised his eyes to him: "Zaccheus,
come down from that tree. Today
I will stay at your house."

Zacchaeus could not believe his ears. He welcomed Jesus into his home with great joy. But some of the people were furious. So Zacchaeus told Jesus, "I will give half of my possessions to the poor. And if I have stolen money from anyone, I will pay it back four times over."

The Unfaithful Woman

John 8:1–11

An excited crowd had gathered before the Temple, yelling, "Look, Jesus, we caught this woman being unfaithful to her husband." Some of them wanted to throw stones at her. "She must be punished! The law says we can stone her!" Jesus said, "You wish to punish her because she has done wrong. Which one of you has never done anything bad? Let that person cast the first stone." They thought about this, and then, one after the other, they left and went home. Jesus said to the woman, "Get up. I will not punish you, either. Go and sin no more."

Jesus
and the Little Children

Mark 10:13–16

While Jesus was speaking, some people were bringing him their children, and the disciples scolded them. But this made Jesus angry: "Let the children come to me. Don't push them away. For the kingdom of God belongs to such as these." And Jesus took them in his arms and blessed them.

The Our Father

Matthew 6:9–13

One day, Jesus confided these words to his friends: "When you pray, speak to God as you would to your own father. Say:

"Our Father, who art in heaven,
hallowed be thy name;
thy kingdom come.
Thy will be done,
on earth as it is in heaven.
Give us this day our daily bread;
and forgive us our trespasses,
as we forgive those who trespass
against us;
and lead us not into temptation,
but deliver us from evil."

Chapter 7

When Jesus Told Stories of the Kingdom

The Beatitudes

Matthew 5:1–12

Great crowds gathered to listen to Jesus.
They had heard about all the good he was doing.
Jesus spoke these extraordinary words to them:
the Beatitudes.

> *"Blessed are the peacemakers,*
> *for they will be called sons of God...*
> *Theirs is the kingdom of heaven...*
> *Rejoice and be glad, for your reward*
> *is great in heaven."*
>
> *(Matthew 5:9, 12)*

The people wondered, "What kingdom is Jesus talking about? Where is it? Who lives there?" In order to explain, Jesus told them beautiful, simple stories called "parables"…

"Blessed are you poor, for yours is the kingdom of God." (Luke 6:20)

The Kingdom of Heaven

Matthew 6:19–21; 7:1–5

Don't try to store up riches here on earth. Instead, store up treasure in heaven by loving God and each other.

Don't judge other people.
What you should do is look first
at the bad things you yourself do,
and then try to be better.

The Mustard Seed

Matthew 13:31–32

The kingdom of God is like
a tiny little mustard seed planted
in a field. It grows as big as a strong tree,
and the birds nest in its branches.

The Sower

Matthew 13:3–9, 18–23

A sower went out to plant seeds.
Some seeds fell on the path, and the birds
made a feast of them! Some seeds fell
on rocky ground. They withered and died.
Some seeds fell among thorns, and they
were choked. Other seeds fell on good soil.
They grew and produced wonderful grain.
The word of God is like these seeds:
you must welcome it into your heart
and allow it to grow.

The Good Samaritan

Luke 10:29–37

A man asked Jesus, "Who is this neighbor I should love?" So Jesus told him a story: "One day, along the road, a traveler was attacked by bandits. They beat him and left him half dead. Some people from that region walked by and saw him, but no one stopped to help him.

"Then a foreigner, a Samaritan, arrived
and stopped. He tenderly cared for
the wounded man and took him to an inn.
'So', Jesus asked, 'who proved to be
a neighbor to the wounded man?'"
The man then understood he must love all
those in need, friends and foreigners alike.

"Go and do likewise." (Luke 10:37)

The Lost Sheep

Luke 15:3–7

God is like a shepherd who has a hundred sheep. One day, he loses one of them in the mountains. He leaves all the others to go look for it. When he finds it, he puts it over his shoulders and carries it back to the sheepfold. He calls to his friends, "Rejoice with me, I have found my lost sheep!"

The Lost Coin

Luke 15:8–10

A woman loses one of her silver coins.
She immediately lights a lamp and sweeps the house,
looking everywhere for it. "There it is! I've found it!"
She quickly calls to her neighbors: "Come celebrate
with me! I've found the coin I lost!"

The Prodigal Son

Luke 15:11–32

A man had two sons. One day, the younger
said to him, "Father, I want to leave home.
Give me my share of the inheritance."
Far from home, he wasted all the money
on foolish things.

   When he had spent everything, he found
himself alone and sad. He was hungry,
so to earn enough to eat, he went to work
tending pigs in the fields.

"I'll go home to my father", he thought, "and work for him as a hired hand. At least I will have bread to eat." The father saw his son arriving in the distance. He ran to meet him and clasped him in his arms. The son said, "Father, I have sinned against God and you; I am no longer worthy to be called your son." But his father said, "My son! I have been waiting for your return since the day you left. Here you are, at last! I've never been so happy!"

"Your brother was dead, and is alive; he was lost, and is found." (Luke 15:32)

"Come, everyone, to celebrate!" the father cried.
"My young son has come home!" But the elder son
sulked: "It's not fair! I've always obeyed my father,
but no one ever celebrated in my honor!" His father
went out to look for him: "All I have is yours.
You are with me always, and I love you. But today,
your brother has returned to us. Come and celebrate
with us."

The Unforgiving Servant

Matthew 18:23–35

The kingdom of God is like that of a good and just king. One of the king's servants owed him a lot of money. When it was time to pay his debt, the servant fell at his feet: "Wait a little while longer. Soon I'll be able to pay it all back, I promise you!" The king was so good that he forgave the man all his debt. A little later, this servant met a friend who owed him a little money.

He grabbed hold of him: "Pay me back right now what you owe me!" His friend begged him, "Wait just a little while. Soon I'll be able to pay you all I owe. I promise!" But the servant had him put in prison.

When the king heard about this, he was very angry. "Should you not have had mercy for your friend, since I had mercy on you?" And he put the servant in prison until he paid back all he owed.

The Two Sons

Matthew 21:28–32

A father had two sons. He said to them, "Go work in my vineyard." "Absolutely not, I won't go", said the first son. But when he saw he had upset his father, he went out to work after all.

The second son answered, "Of course, Father, I'll go right away!" But, in fact, he did not go. Jesus asked those who heard this story, "In your opinion, which one did his father's will?"

The Guests Invited to the Feast

Matthew 22:1–14

"The kingdom of God", said Jesus, "is like a king who prepared a great wedding feast. But, when everything was ready, all those he had invited found an excuse not to come."

The king then told his servants to go out into the street and invite everyone they saw. Jesus said, "God invites all men to the banquet in his kingdom. Blessed are you who are prepared to accept his invitation."

"Blessed are those who are invited to the marriage supper of the Lamb." (Revelation 19:9)

Chapter 8

When Jesus
Performed Miracles

The Wedding at Cana

John 2:1–12

To show that the love of God is stronger than anything, Jesus performed miracles.

He and his mother, Mary, were invited to a wedding at Cana. The wedding feast was delicious. But in the middle of the meal, the wine ran out.

The celebration would be ruined. Mary said
to the servants, "This is my son, Jesus.
Do whatever he tells you." Jesus ordered
the servants, "Fill these jugs with water."
The servants did so, and the water changed
into wine! When the steward tasted it,
not knowing where it had come from,
he said to the bridegroom, "How extraordinary!
You have saved the best wine for last!"

The Healing of the Leper

Mark 1:40–45

A leper fell to his knees at Jesus' feet:
"Look at the sores on my skin. I'm aching.
Please, Jesus, do something to help me."
Jesus looked at the leper with love.
He smiled, laid his hand on him,
and healed him. Jesus said to him,
"Now tell no one anything about this."
But the man went on his way dancing
with joy and telling everyone what Jesus
had done for him.

" 'Be clean.' And immediately
the leprosy left him." (Luke 5:13)

The Healing of the Paralytic

Mark 2:1–12

Jesus entered a house. Everyone came crowding in to hear him. A paralyzed man arrived. He was determined to see Jesus despite the crush of people: "I'm sure this man can heal me!" So his friends lowered his stretcher down from the roof. Jesus said to him, "Your sins are forgiven." But the people said, "Only God can forgive sins!" Then Jesus said, "Rise, pick up your stretcher, and go home." The man stood up. The people could not believe their eyes!

> "We never saw anything like this."
> (Mark 2:12)

The Storm Is Calmed

Mark 4:35–41

It was evening. Jesus was in a boat with
his friends. He was asleep when, suddenly,
the sky grew dark and the wind began to blow.
What a storm! The waves began breaking over
the boat. Jesus' friends were terrified:
"Jesus, help us! Wake up!"

Jesus awoke and ordered the wind and the sea to be quiet. And, all at once, everything became calm. He said to them, "Why are you afraid? Have you no faith?" His friends were amazed: "Who is he, then, that even the wind and the sea obey him?"

"Who then is this?" (Mark 4:41)

The Daughter of Jairus

Mark 5:21–43

A man named Jairus ran up to Jesus and begged him: "My little daughter is dying. Come quickly!" Jesus consoled him: "Do not be afraid, have faith!" When they arrived at Jairus' house, everyone was weeping, for the child had died. "This little girl is not dead", Jesus told them, "she is sleeping." He took her hand and said, "Get up, little girl." And the little girl got up and walked. The people were astounded.

The Multiplication of the Loaves

Mark 6:30–44

One evening, a huge crowd followed
Jesus to a deserted place to listen to him.
His disciples were worried: "Jesus, we must
send them away so they can find food."
Jesus smiled: "You give them something to eat!"

> "You give them something to eat."
> (Mark 6:37)

"All we have are five loaves
of bread and two fish, and there
are thousands of people!" Jesus
took the loaves and the fish
in his hands. He gave thanks
to God, broke the bread
into pieces and divided the fish,
and gave them to his disciples
to distribute to the crowd.
Everyone ate. And there were
still twelve baskets full of pieces
of bread and fish.

They all went home,
their hunger satisfied
and their hearts full of joy!

Peter Walks on the Water

Matthew 14:22–31

Jesus' friends were out in their boat one night. The wind had come up, and waves beat against the boat. All at once, they were terrified: "Look! Someone is walking on the water!" "He's coming toward us—it's a ghost!" But it was Jesus, who said to them, "Take courage, it is I. Don't be afraid." Peter answered, "If it's really you, let me walk over to you on the water." "Come", Jesus said to him. Peter got out of the boat and started to walk on the water. But when he saw how windy it was, he became afraid and began to sink: "Jesus, save me!" With that, Jesus took Peter by the hand: "Why did you not have faith in me?"

"Have courage, it is I; have no fear."
(see Matthew 14:27)

The Canaanite Woman

Matthew 15:21–28

A woman kept crying out to Jesus for help and would not go away. Finally, the disciples had had enough: "Send her away, Jesus. Make her keep quiet!" But she went on repeating, "Jesus, my daughter is sick. Even though I am a foreigner, heal her!" Jesus looked at her and said, "You truly have great faith in me. All will be as you wish." At that moment, her daughter was healed.

The Healing of a Deaf Man

Mark 7:31–37

A man who was deaf and mute was brought to Jesus. He looked at Jesus with eyes full of hope. Jesus placed his hand on the man's ears and on his mouth. He prayed to God, saying, "Ephphatha", which means "Be opened." At these words, the man's ears were opened, and he began to speak clearly. Those who saw this were filled with joy.

"He even makes the deaf hear and the mute speak." (Mark 7:37)

The Blind Bartimaeus

Mark 10:46–52

As Jesus was leaving Jericho with a great crowd of people, a blind beggar named Bartimaeus was sitting by the roadside. When he heard that Jesus was passing by, he cried out, "Jesus, please, have mercy on me!" The people told him to keep quiet, but Bartimaeus only shouted louder. Jesus had him called. In one bound, Bartimaeus leaped toward Jesus. "What do you want me to do for you?" Jesus asked. "I want to see", he said. Jesus replied, "Go, your faith has made you well." And immediately the man's eyes were opened, and he could see. He joined the others and followed Jesus on his way.

"Have courage; rise, he is calling you."
(see Mark 10:49)

The Raising of Lazarus

John 11:1–44

Martha was in tears: "My brother Lazarus has just died. You could have saved him, Jesus, but you've arrived too late." Jesus wept over the death of his friend.

Jesus prayed to God before the tomb of Lazarus. Then he shouted, "Lazarus, come out!" And Lazarus did come out. Many who saw what Jesus did believed in him.

Chapter 9

When Jesus Gave His Life for Us

The Entry into Jerusalem

Mark 11:1–11

Riding a little donkey, Jesus entered Jerusalem to celebrate the feast of Passover. The people rushed to see him. They waved palm branches along his path and covered the ground with their most beautiful cloaks. They cried out, "Hosanna! Blessed is the kingdom that is coming!"

"Hosanna! Blessed is he who comes in the name of the Lord!" (Mark 11:9)

The Merchants in the Temple

Mark 11:15–19

In the Temple, Jesus saw all the merchants counting their money. In great anger, he knocked over their tables and chairs and chased them all out. "The house of God is a house of prayer! But you have turned it into a den of thieves!"

The Last Supper

Luke 22:14–20; John 13:1–15

Jesus knew he was about to die. To celebrate
the Passover, he had a last supper prepared
for his disciples and himself. He took bread,
gave thanks to God, broke the bread, and
gave it to them, saying, "This is my body,
which is given for you. Do this in memory
of me." Then Jesus took a cup of wine,
gave thanks to God, and said,
"Take this and drink it: this is my blood,
which is poured out for you.
Do this in memory of me."

During supper, Jesus poured water into
a basin and washed his disciples' feet.
They were all astonished: "You, our Master,
you want to wash our feet?" Jesus answered
them, "I have come among you in order
to serve you. Now you must follow my
example and wash one another's feet."

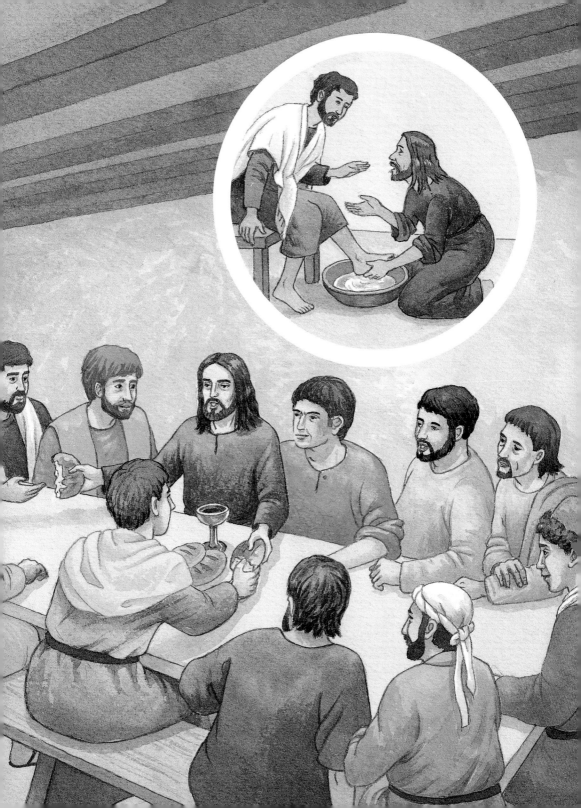

The Arrest of Jesus

Luke 22:21–53

When supper was over, Jesus said,
"Soon I am going to die. One of you
will betray me." They went to the garden
of Gethsemane. Jesus was afraid.
He was sad: "Stay awake. Pray with me."
But the disciples all fell asleep,
and Jesus was left alone to pray.

A group of soldiers came running
toward him. Judas was leading them:
it was he who had betrayed Jesus.
One of the disciples drew his sword to fight,
but Jesus stopped him. The soldiers arrested
Jesus as though he were a common thief
and led him away.

The Trial of Jesus

Mark 14:53—15:20

They took Jesus in the night
to the high priest, who called all
the chief priests, elders, and scribes.
When they could find no real reason
to charge him, some testified that
he wanted to destroy the Temple.
Jesus said nothing to defend himself.
"Are you the Messiah?" the high priest
asked him. "Yes, I am he",
Jesus answered.

Everyone cried out,
"That's blasphemy!* Kill him!"
While Jesus was being tried,
Peter came to the outer courtyard.
Someone recognized him: "You're one
of Jesus' followers!" Peter denied it. Three times
they accused him, and three times he denied
knowing Jesus. Suddenly, Peter heard the cock
crow. Then he remembered the words Jesus had
spoken: "Before the cock crows, you will
deny me three times." And Peter began to weep.

*Blasphemy is anything done or said that shows a lack
 of reverence for God

Jesus was led before Pilate, the Roman governor. But Pilate could not find him guilty of anything. He brought Jesus before the crowd. They all cried out, "Crucify him! Crucify him!" So Pilate, wishing to satisfy the crowd, had Jesus whipped and then handed over to the soldiers to be crucified.

The Crucifixion

Mark 15:21–47; John 19:17–41

Then they made Jesus carry his cross
to the place where he would be crucified.
His mother, Mary, was there with a few
other women and friends. They wept.

"Father, forgive them; for they know
not what they do." (Luke 23:34)

"Father, into yours hands
I commit my spirit." (Luke 23:46)

Jesus died on the cross.

   When evening came, a friend named Joseph
of Arimathea came to take his body.
He wrapped him in a linen sheet and laid
him in a tomb carved out of the rock.
He rolled a very big stone in front of
the entrance and went home in great sadness.

"Truly this man was the Son
of God!" (Mark 15:39)

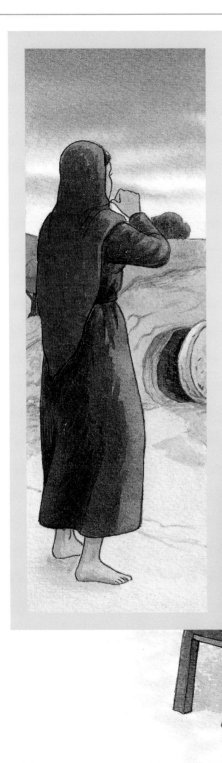

The Resurrection of Jesus

John 20:1–18

Three days later, on Sunday morning, Mary Magdalene, a friend of Jesus, went to the tomb. She saw that the big stone had been rolled away from the entrance. "Jesus' body is gone!" she exclaimed. "Someone has surely stolen it!"

Mary Magdalene rushed to tell Peter and John: "Jesus' body has been taken from the tomb!" Hearing this news, Peter and John ran to the tomb. All they found there were the linen cloths in which Jesus' body had been wrapped.

Mary Magdalene was outside weeping. A man came up to her. He asked her, "Why are you crying?" She thought it was the gardener, but then he said her name, "Mary." At once, she recognized Jesus: "Teacher!"

"I have seen the Lord." (John 20:18)

The Road to Emmaus

Luke 24:13–35

That same day, two friends of Jesus
were walking toward the village of Emmaus.
They were sad. They were talking about
the death of Jesus.

Along the road, a man joined them.
They told him about the death of Jesus.
And this man said that the prophets
had foretold the death and resurrection
of the Messiah. When they arrived in the village,
they asked the stranger to stay with them
for supper. While they were at table,
the man took bread and blessed it.
He broke the bread and gave it to them.

"The Lord has risen indeed!" (Luke 24:34)

At that moment, the two friends
recognized Jesus: He was alive! But then
he vanished … Without a moment's delay,
the two friends set off joyfully back
to Jerusalem. There the apostles told them
the great news: Peter, too, had seen the Lord!
"Jesus is risen!"

Jesus Appears on the Seashore

John 21:1–19

As before, the friends of Jesus went fishing on the Sea of Tiberias. At dawn, their nets were still empty! A man called to them from the shore, "Have you caught anything to eat?" "Not a single fish", they answered. So the man said to them, "Cast your net over the right side of the boat. You'll have a good catch!" And so they did; the net was almost too full.

John recognized the man: "It's Jesus!" At that, Peter jumped into the water to go to Jesus.

They prepared a big meal with all of the fish they had caught. Then Jesus turned to Peter three times, asking, "Peter, do you love me?" "Yes, Jesus", he answered, "you know that I love you." Jesus said to him, "Peter, you must be the shepherd, now, and take care of my sheep."

Chapter 10

When the Spirit of God Sends a Mission

The Ascension
and the Choosing of Matthias

Acts 1:6–26

Jesus gathered his disciples on a mountain.
They asked him, "When will your kingdom come?"
"I cannot tell you that now", Jesus replied, "but soon
you will receive the power of the Holy Spirit. Then
you will be my witnesses to the ends of the earth."
When he had said this, Jesus disappeared into the sky.

Without Judas, who had betrayed Jesus, there were now only eleven apostles left. "There must be twelve of us, as before", said Peter. They all prayed together and then chose Matthias, who had been a follower of Jesus from the start.

"You shall be my witnesses." (Acts 1:8)

Pentecost

Acts 2:1–11

On the day of Pentecost, the disciples of Jesus were gathered in a house in Jerusalem. Suddenly, they heard a noise like a strong wind and saw what looked like flames coming down to rest on them. It was the Holy Spirit promised by Jesus and sent by God. The apostles began to speak in different languages.

There were people in Jerusalem from many
different countries, but they could all understand
what the apostles were saying.

Peter, filled with the Holy Spirit, proclaimed,
"This Jesus, whom you crucified, has been
raised up by God. We have all seen him!"

"God raised up this Jesus, and of that
we all are witnesses." (see Acts 2:32)

The First Christian Communities

Acts 2:42–47; 4:32–35

Those who believed in Jesus liked to meet together. They gathered in each other's houses to hear the apostles proclaim the good news.

They listened to the apostles speak about Jesus. They prayed and broke bread together, as Jesus had asked them to do. They also shared everything they owned so that no one would be in need, because everyone is precious in the eyes of God.

The Miracle of the Lame Beggar and the Stoning of Stephen

Acts 3:1–10; 5:12–16; 7:54–60; 8:1

A lame man sat in front of the Temple, begging for money. Peter said to him, "I have no money, but what I do have I give you: in the name of Jesus, get up and walk." With that, the man got up, jumping for joy and praising God. Everyone was filled with amazement. Many people came to the apostles to be healed. Those who had condemned Jesus to death were very displeased.

Stephen was a friend of Jesus who helped others and took care of the poor. When he spoke, everyone stopped to listen to him. But when he said he could see Jesus, whom they had killed, standing next to God in heaven, the scribes and elders were enraged and stoned him. As Stephen died, he prayed, "Lord, do not hold this sin against them."

"In the name of Jesus ... walk." (Acts 3:6)

Saul's Conversion

Acts 9:1–22

Saul was among those who agreed to Stephen's death. He continued tracking down those who believed in Jesus. One day, on the road to Damascus, he was stunned by a dazzling light. He heard a voice saying, "Saul, I am Jesus. Why are you persecuting me?" When he got back up, he was blind. He was led to Damascus to a friend of Jesus named Ananias, who took care of him. When Ananias placed his hands on Saul's eyes, he regained his sight. Ananias baptized him. His new name was Paul. At once, Paul set out to proclaim the good news of Jesus.

Peter and Cornelius

Acts 10

One day, Peter had a vision that
he did not understand. Far away from
there, Cornelius, a Roman soldier,
also had a vision, in which he was told
to go to Peter. A little while later,
Peter and Cornelius met in person.

They had nothing in common, and yet they greeted each other like brothers. Cornelius wished to be baptized. But Peter hesitated: Did he have the right to baptize a foreigner, an enemy soldier? But then Peter understood his vision: Jesus had come to save all men!

The Great Council of Jerusalem

Acts 9:26–31; 11:1–18; 13:1–3

All the apostles gathered in Jerusalem. Barnabas introduced them to Paul. Some were astonished to see that their old enemy had become one of them. Paul wanted to preach about Jesus to people everywhere. Peter, too, agreed to proclaim Jesus to men of every race. They prayed with the other apostles, asking God to help them find the best way to announce the good news. Paul was sent on a mission with Barnabas. Together, they set off to carry the good news to the four corners of the earth!

The Journeys of Paul

Acts 13:13–52; 16:11–15; 18:1–3; 19:1–7; 27:13–44

Paul traveled tirelessly, going from village to village to speak about Jesus. And what adventures he had along the way! Those who accepted the good news of Jesus were called Christians. Paul worked and prayed with them. Sometimes, people welcomed Paul. Other times, they made fun of him or chased him away or even wanted to kill him.

"Christ ... lives in me." (Galatians 2:20)

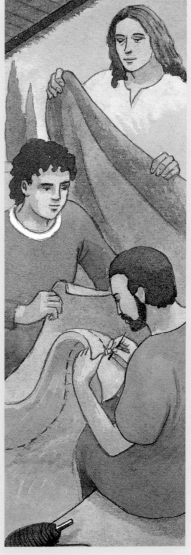

Near the island of Crete, Paul's boat was caught in a storm. He was shipwrecked, and he almost drowned. Everywhere he went, Paul baptized men, women, and children. A woman named Lydia invited Paul to stay, and there he rested a while. He worked with his companions. He was a tentmaker. In the synagogues, the Jewish houses of prayer, he explained the word of God.

Paul's Letters

1 Corinthians 13; Acts 21:27—28:30

Paul did not want the new Christians to feel alone. So he wrote them long letters full of advice to encourage them to grow in faith, in hope, and, most especially, in love.

When the Christians received a letter, they would take good care of it and read it over and over together. The apostles Peter, James, and John also wrote very beautiful letters.

"If I speak in the tongues of men and of angels, but have not love, I am a noisy gong or a clanging cymbal...

"If I give away all I have... but have not love, I gain nothing...

"Love is patient and kind... it does not rejoice at wrong, but rejoices in the right. It... endures all things."

(1 Corinthians 13:1-7)

"It is no longer I who live, but Christ who lives in me." (Galatians 2:20)

One day, Paul was arrested.
Soldiers took him to Rome
to be tried. And this was
to be the end of his journey.

The Heavenly Jerusalem

Revelation 7:9–12; 21:1–4; 22:14–17

The apostle John had a beautiful vision of heaven.
He saw people from every race and nation worshipping
God together in perfect happiness forever.
After the death of the apostles, including Paul,
the number of Christians continued to grow.
As in the vision of John, men and women
from all different countries came to believe
in the saving power of Jesus. The Lord Jesus
was calling them all to come, to enter
his holy city, his Church, and to be
his people, his family, with whom
he would dwell forever.

"Behold, I am with you always, until the close of the age." (Matthew 28:20)

Abel *pp. 16–17*

Abel was the second son of Adam* and Eve.* He tended a flock of sheep from which he offered the first lambs to God. God approved of his offering and looked with favor on Abel. His brother Cain* was very jealous of this. He lured Abel into the fields, where he attacked and killed him.

Abraham *pp. 24–26, 35*

The head of a clan of shepherds in Mesopotamia, Abraham was chosen by God to be the father of the faithful. God promised him land and numerous descendants. Abraham left his country with his family and his flocks to go to the land God gave him, Canaan.* Though he was very old and childless, God gave him a son, Isaac.* Abraham always obeyed and trusted in God.

Adam *pp. 12–16*

Adam was the first man, molded by God from the earth. His name means "red earth". God created woman, Eve,* from Adam's rib. They both lived in the garden God gave them. One day, tempted by the snake, they disobeyed God and ate the forbidden fruit from the tree of the knowledge of good and evil. They were forced to leave the garden. Thus began man's wandering over the earth. Jesus is the new Adam, obedient even to death. Through his Resurrection, he conquered death.

Amos *pp. 76, 82*

Amos lived about the year 750 B.C. in the Northern Kingdom of Israel, a rich and prosperous land at the time. He was a prophet, a messenger of God. He denounced the injustice of the rich toward the poor and announced God's punishment of Israel if men did not change their ways.

Ananias *p. 217*

Ananias was a Christian of Damascus, in modern-day Syria. He heard the voice of Jesus sending him to see Paul,* who persecuted the Christians. Ananias welcomed and healed Paul, who had been blinded after a vision of the risen Christ, and then baptized him.

Andrew *p. 122*

Andrew and his brother, Simon Peter,* were fishermen on the Sea of Galilee. One day, Jesus called him to be his disciple. Leaving his nets and his boat, he followed him and brought along his brother, Simon Peter. They both became apostles of Jesus.

Ark of the Covenant
pp. 49, 55, 65, 69

After receiving the Ten Commandments from God engraved on tablets of stone, Moses* placed them in a large chest of wood covered in gold and surmounted by two golden angels, as God had instructed. This Ark was the sign of the presence of God among his people. It accompanied the Hebrews during their long march through the desert until their arrival in Canaan.* King David* then had it brought in triumph to Jerusalem,* and his son, King Solomon,* had a sumptuous temple built to house it.

Ascension *pp. 208–9*

Forty days after his Resurrection, Jesus went with some of his disciples to the Mount of Olives, near Jerusalem.* After promising to send them the Holy Spirit so that they could witness to him throughout the world, Jesus was taken up to heaven and disappeared from their sight.

Babel *pp. 22-23*

The descendants of Noah* wanted to build a gigantic tower to reach the sky. God stopped their work by making them speak in different languages. The dispersion of man throughout the world is traced back to this moment. In Hebrew, *babel* means "confusion".

Babylon *pp. 83, 84*

Babylon was a very ancient city on the banks of the Euphrates, in modern Iraq. In 587 B.C., under King Nebuchadnezzar II, that is where the Hebrews were deported after the destruction of Jerusalem. The memory of this event made Babylon a symbol of evil in the Bible.

Barnabas *pp. 220-21*

Barnabas means "son of encouragement" and is the name given by the disciples to Joseph, a Jew from Cyprus who became a Christian. It was he who welcomed the newly converted Paul.* He accompanied him on his voyages in Asia Minor. He was sent to Antioch. After a disagreement with Paul, Barnabas left him to evangelize Cyprus.

Bartimaeus *pp. 180-81*

Bartimaeus, the son of Timaeus, was a blind beggar who lived at the gates of the city of Jericho.* One day, as Jesus was passing by, Bartimaeus called to him, "Jesus, Son of David, have mercy on me!" He was healed by Jesus and then followed him.

Bathsheba *pp. 66-67*

Bathsheba was the wife of Uriah,* a general in the army of King David.* Seduced by her beauty, David had Uriah sent to war to have him killed so that he could marry Bathsheba. When God saw David's remorse for this crime, he forgave him and gave Bathsheba and David a son, Solomon.*

Beatitudes *p. 142*

To a large crowd that followed him, Jesus taught the way to true happiness, that of the poor and the humble, not that of material wealth and power. This Sermon on the Mount is presented as the law of a new covenant in which love is the first rule.

Bethlehem *pp. 102, 106, 108*

Bethlehem is a little town in Judea, to the south of Jerusalem. It was the hometown of King David.* David's descendant Joseph* and his wife, Mary,* went there to be enrolled in the census ordered by the Roman emperor. It was in this town that Jesus was born.

Cain *pp.16-17*

Cain was the eldest son of Adam* and Eve.* He tilled the soil. He was jealous of his brother Abel,* a shepherd, and killed him. God condemned Cain to be a nomad, wandering the face of the earth. But when Cain repented, God placed a sign on him to protect him from anyone who wished to attack him.

Cana *pp. 164-65*

It was in this village in Galilee that Jesus performed his first miracle by changing water into wine at a wedding feast.

Canaan *p. 54*

When God made a covenant with Abraham,* he promised him descendants and a land in which to settle. This was the Promised Land, where Moses* led the Hebrew people after their departure from Egypt.* It is the land where Jesus lived, in the modern-day state of Israel and Palestine.

Commandments (the Ten) *pp. 46–49*

Shortly after the Hebrews' departure from Egypt and the crossing of the Red Sea, God gave Moses* a law on Mount Sinai. Engraved on tablets of stone, these ten rules, called in Greek the *Decalogue*, sealed the covenant between God and man. The Hebrew people based their way of life on them.

Cornelius *pp. 218-19*

Cornelius was a Roman centurion who lived in the coastal city of Caesarea. He respected and loved the God of Israel. An angel of the Lord appeared to him, asking him to go see the apostle Peter.* Cornelius asked Peter to baptize his whole family. This was the first time that non-Jews received baptism.

Creation *pp. 10–13*

The creation of the world is recounted in two stories in Genesis, the first book of the Bible. These stories, written between the tenth and sixth centuries B.C., are not scientific accounts. Rather, they convey a spiritual and religious vision of a world in which God entrusts creation to mankind.

Damascus *pp. 216-17*

Located in modern Syria, Damascus is one of the most ancient cities of the world. In the time of Jesus, Jewish communities already existed there. The gospel was proclaimed very early in Damascus, and a small local church had formed before the arrival of Paul.* It was on the road to Damascus that Jesus appeared to Paul in a vision.

Daniel *pp. 76, 84–87*

His name means "God is my judge." Daniel, a young Israelite, served at the court of Babylon. He interpreted the king's dreams and predicted the future of the empire. He remained faithful to his religion even though it was against the law of the land. For this, he was thrown into a lions' den, but he emerged unscathed, singing and praising God.

Darius *pp. 84, 86-87*

King of Babylon in the sixth century B.C., Darius is mentioned in the Bible as the "son of Ahasuerus, of the race of the Medes", but there is no historical record of this. Darius chose Daniel,* a young Israelite, as minister. It was due to Daniel that Darius allowed the Jews to practice their religion in complete freedom.

David *pp. 60–68, 72, 98*

David was a shepherd of Bethlehem,* chosen by God and designated by the prophet Samuel* to become the second king of Israel.* He succeeded King Saul. He was a musician and a poet, a talented politician and a glorious general. He made Jerusalem* his political and religious capital. He wrote numerous psalms in praise of God. The Messiah was to be born of his descendants. Jesus is called "the son of David".

Delilah *pp. 56–57*

This Philistine woman seduced Samson,* a strong Hebrew warrior. The Philistines were enemies of the Hebrews. While Samson slept, Delilah cut his hair, the sign of his consecration to God and the source of his superhuman strength. She then handed Samson over to the Philistines.

Egypt
pp. 29, 32–42, 45, 109

Following a great famine, the sons of Jacob* sought refuge in Egypt. They were called the Hebrews. A few centuries later, Pharaoh* reduced them to slavery. It was Moses* who freed his people and brought them out of Egypt. The crossing of the Red Sea was their passage from slavery to freedom.

Elijah
pp. 76–78

Elijah was a great prophet in the Northern Kingdom of Israel in the ninth century B.C. He fought against the prophets of the gods of Baal. At the end of his life, he was carried to heaven in a chariot of fire. Elisha* was his successor.

Elizabeth
pp. 100-101

Elizabeth was the wife of Zechariah.* They were childless until the day the angel Gabriel* announced to Zechariah that he would have a son named John, who would prepare the coming of Christ. When Mary* was expecting Jesus, she visited her cousin Elizabeth. As soon as Elizabeth saw her cousin, her baby leaped in her womb.

Emmaus
p. 201

It was on the road to this village not far from Jerusalem* that Jesus appeared to two of the disciples on Easter evening after his Resurrection. After walking and talking with them, he broke bread. It was with this gesture that the disciples recognized him. Jesus then disappeared from their sight.

Esau
p. 26

Esau was the twin brother of Jacob* and the son of Isaac,* but he was considered the elder and the rightful successor of Isaac. Jacob usurped his place through trickery.

Eve
pp. 13–16

Her name means "the living woman". She is also called "the mother of all the living". Along with Adam,* she ate the forbidden fruit of the tree of the knowledge of good and evil. They were both forced to leave the Garden of Eden as a result.

Flood (the)
pp. 18–21

The story of the Flood is told in Genesis, the first book of the Bible. Water covered the whole earth, and all creation was drowned, except for Noah, his family, and a pair of every species of living creature, who took refuge in the ark.* After forty days, the waters receded, and life could begin anew. A rainbow, like a bridge between heaven and earth, was the sign of the covenant between God and man.

Gabriel (the angel)
pp. 98–99

Gabriel was the angel, a messenger of God, who announced the coming of the Messiah. He appeared first to the prophet Daniel* in the Old Testament, then to Zechariah,* the father of John the Baptist,* but above all to Mary* to announce that she was to be the mother of the Messiah, Jesus the Savior.

Galilee (the Sea of)
pp. 170–71, 176–77, 204–5

The Sea of Galilee, also called the Sea of Tiberias, was an important center of fishing and commerce, known for its powerful storms. It was on the banks of this sea that Jesus called Peter,* Andrew,* James,* and John.* It was also there that Jesus calmed the storm and called Peter to come to him on the water.

Gethsemane (the garden of) *pp. 190–91*

This garden is located outside Jerusalem at the foot of its ramparts. Jesus often withdrew there with his disciples to pray. It was here that he was arrested on the eve of his death. It may also have been the place where he ascended to heaven forty days after his Resurrection.

Goliath *pp. 62–63*

Goliath was a Philistine soldier, an enemy of the Hebrews remarkable for his gigantic stature. While still young, David took up his challenge to single combat and killed Goliath with his slingshot.

Herod *pp. 106, 108–9, 111*

Herod the Great was the governor of Galilee. Worried for his throne on hearing of the birth of Jesus, he ordered the massacre of all the newborn boys in Bethlehem.* His was a bloody reign of absolute power.

Hosea *pp. 76, 81*

Hosea was a prophet of Israel around the year 750 B.C. Above all, he denounced the worship of Baal, a false god whose cult was widespread at the time. Despite all, Hosea believed God still loved his unfaithful people. He compared God to a mother who treats her child with tenderness or a father who continues to love a rebellious son.

Isaac *pp. 26, 35*

Isaac was the son God had promised to Abraham* and Sarah* in their old age. His name means "God smiles". To test Abraham, God asked him to sacrifice this promised son, but he saved Isaac by sending a ram to be sacrificed in his place.

Isaiah *pp. 76, 94*

The greatest of all the prophets, Isaiah lived in the eighth century B.C. in the kingdom of Judea, south of Israel. He warned against injustice and a lack of trust in God. He announced the coming of the Savior, "Emmanuel", which means "God with us".

Israel *pp. 76, 83–84*

Israel was the name originally given to Jacob.* It is the name given to his descendants when they settled in Canaan,* the Promised Land. The Northern Kingdom was called the "Kingdom of Israel" when it separated from the Southern Kingdom around 933 B.C. The name of Israel later extended to include all the Hebrew people, the "Israelites".

Jacob *pp. 26–27, 29, 35*

Jacob was the son of Isaac* and the grandson of Abraham.* He was chosen by God to supplant his twin brother, Esau,* and had twelve sons, who formed the twelve tribes of Israel.* He was given the name Israel after wrestling with the angel of God. "Israel" means "one who struggles with God".

James *pp. 129, 225*

The son of Zebedee, James and his brother, John,* were fishermen on the Sea of Galilee.* Jesus called both of them, and they followed him immediately. James was one of the apostles closest to Jesus. He later became one of the heads of the early Church. He died a martyr in Jerusalem.*

Jeremiah *pp. 76, 80*

A prophet in the seventh to the sixth century B.C., Jeremiah predicted imminent misfortunes for the people unless they changed their lives. Jerusalem* was eventually occupied and destroyed by Nebuchadnezzar, the king of Babylon,* and the inhabitants of Jerusalem were deported to Babylon.

Jericho *pp. 54–55, 134*

This city in the valley of the Jordan,* to the north-east of Jerusalem,* was taken by the Hebrews, who, after marching seven times around the city, saw its walls fall down before them. Jesus visited Jericho several times to heal the sick and the blind. It was there that he met Zacchaeus,* a rich tax collector who converted.

Jerusalem *pp. 64–65, 69, 83, 106, 112–13, 186, 203, 210, 220*

Built on Mount Zion, Jerusalem is a very ancient city. David* took it over around the year 1000 B.C. He made it his capital and moved the Ark of the Covenant* there. His son Solomon* built the Temple. In 587 B.C., Nebuchadnezzar destroyed the city and deported the population to Babylon.* Jerusalem became the symbol of the homeland in which the exiled Jews placed all their hopes. It is described by the prophets as the holy city. Jerusalem would later become once again the great spiritual center of the Jews. Many of the episodes in the public life of Jesus took place here, and it was the place of his crucifixion. To Christians, Jerusalem is the symbol of the city of God, the "heavenly Jerusalem".

Jesse *pp. 60–61*

Jesse was a rich landowner who lived in Bethlehem.* He had eight sons, the youngest of whom, David,* became king of Israel.

Job *pp. 92–93*

Job was a rich and happy man who suddenly lost everything. He cried to God in outrage, but he did not blame him; he continued to hope. God at last gave him a new life. The Book of Job, in the form of a tragic poem, explores the meaning of misfortune and suffering.

John (the Baptist) *pp. 115–16, 128*

John the Baptist was born when his mother, Elizabeth,* was already very old. His birth was announced to his father, Zechariah,* by the angel Gabriel.* As a young man, he withdrew to the desert, where he lived on locusts and wild honey. He announced the coming of Jesus. This is why he is considered the last of the prophets. It was he who baptized Jesus in the waters of the Jordan* and was imprisoned shortly thereafter by King Herod Antipas, who had him beheaded.

John (the Evangelist) *pp. 129, 199, 225, 226*

John was the youngest apostle, "the one whom Jesus loved". He was present at the foot of the cross. Jesus entrusted his mother, Mary,* to him. On Easter morning, John along with Peter* discovered the empty tomb, and he immediately believed in the Resurrection of Jesus. His life ended in Ephesus.

Jonah *pp. 76, 88–91*

God sent Jonah to Nineveh* to tell its inhabitants to convert. But Jonah did not want to go and fled on a ship. A great storm at sea sent him straight into the belly of a whale, where he spent three days begging God's forgiveness. When at last thrown back onto the shore, he left for Nineveh. The inhabitants converted, and God withdrew his threat to destroy the city.

Jordan River *pp. 115–16*

The Jordan runs through the entire Promised Land from north to south, crossing the Sea of Galilee* before flowing into the Dead Sea. It was in the Jordan that John* baptized Jesus.

Joseph (husband of Mary)

pp. 98–99, 102–3, 105, 109, 111–14

Joseph, a descendant of David,* was a carpenter of Nazareth* engaged to Mary.* The angel Gabriel* appeared to him in a dream to announce the birth of Jesus. Joseph became the adoptive father of Jesus. He led Mary and Jesus into Egypt to escape the massacre of children ordered by Herod.* We find him again, when Jesus was twelve, on a pilgrimage to Jerusalem during which he and Mary found their lost son, Jesus, in the Temple explaining the Scriptures to the great religious scholars.

Joseph (son of Jacob) *pp. 27–29*

The son of Jacob* and Rachel, Joseph was his father's favorite. His jealous brothers sold him to Egyptian traders. He later became Pharaoh's* prime minister, in charge of the stewardship of the kingdom, who saved the country from a great famine. When his brothers arrived in Egypt seeking refuge from the famine, he welcomed them and forgave them their wicked deed.

Judas *pp. 191, 209*

Judas was one of the twelve apostles chosen by Jesus. He betrayed Jesus to the high priests and, afterward, hung himself in despair.

Lazarus *pp. 182–83*

Lazarus was Jesus' friend, the brother of Martha* and Mary,* who lived in Bethany, near Jerusalem.

He had fallen ill, died, and been placed in a tomb by the time Jesus arrived. In a prefigurement of his own Resurrection, Jesus raised him back to life.

Lydia *p. 223*

Lydia was a rich merchant-woman in the trade of purple dye. She lived in Philippi in Macedonia. She converted after hearing Paul* preach. She then invited Paul and his companions to stay with her during their visit to that city.

Magi *p. 106*

The Magi, or the Magi kings, is the name given to the wise men who came from the East to adore the Baby Jesus. They followed a new star, which had appeared in the sky, the sign of the birth of a king. They brought him gold, incense, and myrrh. Their names—Gaspar, Melchior, and Balthazar—do not appear in the Gospels but are part of a tradition dating to the seventh century.

Martha and Mary

pp. 130–31, 182

Martha and Mary were the two sisters of Lazarus.* They lived in Bethany, near Jerusalem, and were close friends of Jesus. One day when Jesus was having supper with them, Martha complained at having to do everything herself while Mary listened to Jesus. He then explained that Mary had chosen the better part, and it would not be taken from her.

Mary *pp. 98–103, 105, 109, 111–14, 164, 195, 210*

Mary of Nazareth* was engaged to Joseph* when the angel Gabriel* appeared to her to announce she would become the mother of the Savior. She said Yes to the angel. At the foot of the cross, Jesus entrusted her to John,* his beloved disciple, thus making her the mother of all his disciples. She is venerated by the Church as the Mother of God.

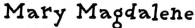

Mary Magdalene

pp. 198–200

Mary Magdalene is named after the town of Magdala, where she lived on the coast of the Sea of Galilee.* It was there that Jesus met her and chased out her seven demons. She was present at the foot of the cross and at Jesus' deposition in the tomb. The following day, having come to embalm his corpse, she found the empty tomb. She was the first person to whom the risen Jesus appeared. She ran at once to announce the news to the disciples.

Matthew *p. 123*

Matthew was originally named Levi. He lived in Capernaum on the coast of the Sea of Galilee,* where he worked as a tax collector for the Roman occupier. Jesus called him as he was sitting at his desk, and Matthew followed him immediately. After the death of Jesus, he wrote one of the Gospels. He is thought to have evangelized Ethiopia and died a martyr.

Matthias *p. 209*

Matthias was a follower of Jesus from the start. After the death of Jesus, the apostles chose him to replace Judas,* who had betrayed Jesus. He is thought to have evangelized Turkey and died a martyr.

Miriam *see p. 33*

Miriam was the elder sister of Moses.* When her mother placed Moses in a basket on the Nile to protect him from the massacre ordered by Pharaoh,* Miriam hid in the reeds to watch over him. She was by Moses' side during the people's long march through the desert.

Moses *pp. 33–36, 38, 40, 43–46, 48–49, 51*

When the Hebrews were slaves in Egypt,* Moses was saved from the massacre ordered by Pharaoh* by being hidden in a basket left on the Nile. He was found by a princess and raised as an adopted son. In rebellion against the enslavement of his people, he was forced to flee into the desert. There the Lord spoke to him and sent him to save the Hebrews from their slavery.

After many great difficulties, Moses led the Hebrew people to the Promised Land. He met God face to face on Mount Sinai. Through his mediation, God formed a covenant with the Hebrews and entrusted the Ten Commandments* to him. Moses was never to enter the Promised Land of Canaan,* but he contemplated it from atop Mount Nebo, where, having fulfilled his mission, he died.

The Jewish people consider Moses the greatest of the prophets and patriarchs.

Naaman *p. 79*

Naaman was an army general of Damascus* in the ninth century B.C. When he caught leprosy, he sought out the prophet Elisha* for a cure. Elisha had no hesitation in coming to the aid of a foreigner. Once healed, Naaman promised to sacrifice to no other god than the God of the Hebrews.

Nathan *p. 67*

Nathan was a prophet around the year 1000 B.C. in the time of King David.* He vehemently reproached the king for sending Uriah* to his death in combat in order to marry his wife, Bathsheba.* He advised David throughout his reign and encouraged the succession of David's son Solomon* to the throne.

Nazareth *pp. 98, 111, 120*

Nazareth is a village in Galilee* and the birthplace of Mary.* Joseph* was a carpenter there. They lived in this village before the birth of Jesus and returned there after the flight into Egypt.* It was here that Jesus grew up. As an adult, he returned to announce that he was the Messiah, but the population of Nazareth rejected him.

Nineveh *pp. 88, 91*

An ancient city of Assyria (modern-day Iraq) on the banks of the Tigris, Nineveh is often cited in the Bible as an accursed place. Faced with the evil of its inhabitants, God sent the prophet Jonah.* The entire city repented and converted, and God pardoned Nineveh.

Noah *pp. 18–22*

Noah was a descendant of Seth, the third son of Adam* and Eve.* He and his family were righteous and loved God. When God decided to send the Flood* upon the earth, he chose Noah to build a boat, the ark, in which he saved a pair of each species of living creature.

Passover *pp. 37–42, 186, 188, 198–200*

The Jewish feast of Passover commemorates the liberation of the Hebrews from their slavery in Egypt.* The paschal feast recalls the meal eaten in haste by the Hebrews before starting their long march through the desert to the Promised Land. Like all Jews, Jesus and his disciples celebrated the feast of Passover. It was during a Passover meal that Jesus instituted the Eucharist. For Christians, Jesus is the paschal lamb, whose death and Resurrection free us from evil and sin and open to us life that is stronger than death.

Paul *pp. 216–17, 220–26*

Paul, initially called Saul, was a Jew and a Roman citizen who persecuted the first Christians. He was present when Stephen* was stoned. He was abruptly converted as he made his way to Damascus* to persecute the Christians there. Jesus appeared to him in a brilliant light, which knocked him to the ground and blinded him for a time. Saul was baptized and took the name Paul. He became a vigorous defender of the Christian faith. Paul traveled throughout Asia Minor and Greece, where he founded Christian communities to whom he later wrote numerous letters. He was arrested and sent to Rome, where he was beheaded around the year 65.

Pentecost *pp. 210–11*

Pentecost comes from a Greek word meaning "fifty". Fifty days after Easter, the apostles received the gift of the Holy Spirit. They went into the streets of Jerusalem* proclaiming the death and Resurrection of Jesus.

Peter *pp. 122, 128–29, 176–77, 193, 199, 204–5, 209, 214, 218–20, 225*

Known as Simon, he was a fisherman on the Sea of Galilee* with his brother, Andrew.* He was the first to recognize Jesus as the Christ, the Son of God. Jesus gave him the name of Peter, which means "rock", to indicate that he would be the rock upon which the Church would be built. Following Pentecost,* Peter proclaimed the living Christ in Jerusalem* and then in Rome, despite his repeated arrests. He wrote letters of encouragement to various Christian communities. He died a martyr in Rome sometime around the year 64 or 67.

Pharaoh *pp. 29, 32, 35–37, 39*

The Pharaoh was the king of Egypt. He was considered by the Egyptians to be a god. At the time of Moses,* the Pharaoh was Ramses II. When Moses brought his people out of Egypt by crossing the Red Sea on dry land, God closed the sea over the pursuing Egyptians. God was victorious over Pharaoh and his entire army. To the Hebrews, Pharaoh represented evil.

Pilate *p. 194*

Pontius Pilate was the governor of Judea, the representative of the Roman emperor, at the time of Jesus. When Jesus was arrested, he was sent

before Pilate, who questioned him and, finding no reason to condemn him, wished to release him. In the end, he gave in to the pressure of the crowd, who demanded Jesus' death, and had him crucified.

Queen of Sheba *pp. 72–73*
News of the wisdom of King Solomon* reached the ears of the queen of Sheba. She traveled from Ethiopia to Jerusalem* with all of her ambassadors to consult him. Solomon answered all of her questions without difficulty. Before the wisdom of Solomon and the beauty and richness of his palace and the Temple, the queen of Sheba blessed the God of Solomon.

Samson *pp. 56–57*
God endowed Samson with superhuman strength. But one day, a Philistine from the camp of the enemy, Delilah,* took away his strength by cutting his hair. She handed him over to the Philistines, who put out his eyes. Samson later had his revenge and saved his people by pulling down the columns of the temple. Three thousand Philistines were crushed under its stones. Samson, too, died in the collapse of the building.

Samuel *pp. 58–61*
Samuel was a very great prophet. As a child, he lived in the temple of Shiloh with the old priest Eli. One night, God called Samuel to entrust him with the mission of speaking in God's name. When Samuel grew up, God gave him the task of designating the king of Israel. It was Samuel who chose David* from among the sons of Jesse.*

Sarah *pp. 24–26*
Sarah was the wife of Abraham.* When God promised Abraham he would have a son and many descendants, Sarah laughed because she was already very old. But she gave birth to Isaac.*

Silas *p. 221*
Silas was one of the first Christians of Jerusalem.* He was the faithful friend of Paul,* whom he was chosen to assist and accompany on his voyages. With Paul, he founded the Churches of Thessalonica and Corinth, in Greece.

Simon *pp. 126–27*
There are many Simons in the New Testament: the two apostles, Simon Peter* and Simon the Zealot; Simon of Cyrene, who helped Jesus carry his cross; Simon was also the name of the brother of the Lord and of Simon the leper, at whose home Mary of Bethany poured perfume on Jesus' head. Another Simon, the Pharisee, invited Jesus to supper where, there too, a woman came to bathe the feet of Jesus in perfume and dry them with her hair.

Sinai (Mount) *p. 46*
Mount Sinai, where Moses met the Lord face to face and received the Ten Commandments, is located on the Sinai Peninsula in Egypt. It was from the desert of Sinai that the Hebrew people set off when they left Egypt.

Solomon *pp. 67–73*
Solomon was the son of David.* The king of Israel from 970 to 933 B.C., he was renowned for his great wisdom. His reign marked a period of peace and prosperity for the country. He had a magnificent Temple built in Jerusalem* to house the Ark of the Covenant.* This sumptuous temple brought new luster to the Israelites' religion. The end of Solomon's reign was shaken by revolts. Following his death, the kingdom of Israel split in two.

Stephen *pp. 215–16*

Stephen was a Jew of Greek origin living in Jerusalem.* He converted to Christianity and became one of the first deacons. He assisted the apostles in serving the community. He proclaimed his faith loudly and strongly and told the elders and the priests in the Council that he could see Jesus, whom they had killed, standing at God's side in heaven. This caused such an outrage that they stoned him to death. He was the first Christian martyr.

Timothy *p. 221*

Timothy, a Jew of Jerusalem,* became a Christian and a disciple of Paul,* with whom he made several voyages in Greece. Paul entrusted the Church of Ephesus to him. Two of Paul's letters—in which he described the role of the leader of a Christian community—were written to Timothy. Like Paul, Timothy was imprisoned. Once freed, he became one of the first successors of the apostles.

Titus *p. 221*

Titus was of Greek origin. He converted to Christianity and became a disciple and collaborator of Paul.* He was put in charge of organizing the Church of Crete. One of Paul's letters was addressed to Titus, advising him about the founding principles of the Church of Crete.

Uriah *pp. 66–67*

Uriah was a soldier in the army of King David.* He was married to Bathsheba,* a very beautiful woman who had attracted the attentions of David. In order to have Bathsheba as his own, David had Uriah sent to the front line of battle to be killed.

Zacchaeus *pp. 134–35*

In the city of Jericho,* Zacchaeus was the chief tax collector on behalf of the Roman occupiers. He was very rich. One day, Jesus came to Jericho, but Zacchaeus, who was very short, could not manage to see him through the crowd, so he climbed a tree to get a better view. Jesus called to him and asked to stay at his house. Zacchaeus received him with joy and converted to Christianity. He returned his dishonestly earned money and gave half of his wealth to the poor.

Cover design: Élisabeth Hebert

Layout design: Michèle Bisgambiglia

Layout: Jean-Marc Richard

Original French edition:
La Bible pour les Enfants

© 2010 by Mame, Paris
© 2011 by Ignatius Press, San Francisco • Magnificat USA LLC, New York
ISBN Ignatius Press 978-1-58617-659-4 • ISBN Magnificat 978-1-936260-27-0
Library of Congress Control Number 2011923601
The trademark MAGNIFICAT depicted in this publication is used under license
from and is the exclusive property of Magnificat Central Service Team, Inc.,
A Ministry to Catholic Women, and may not be used without its written consent.

Printed by Tien Wah Press, Singapore
Printed on July 4, 2011
Job Number MGN 11007
Printed in Singapore in compliance with the Consumer Protection Safety Act, 2008.